# THE VIRTUES OF KITTENS

## The Virtues of Kittens

Of all of the pets you might ponder owning, the kitten has possibly the most virtues and the least drawbacks. Certainly it is the most convenient pet to have around the home, for it is very undemanding in its needs, yet offers companionship. Its upkeep is minimal, and it will not annoy your neighbors as might a dog or large and raucous parrot. You will not need to take kitty out for a daily walk, for if it has access to a yard or garden, it will prefer to exercise itself. At the same time, if you wish to have a stroll round the garden, kitty will be more than happy to go along as well.

There is virtually no training to attend to with kittens; and grooming, even with longcoated

Tortoiseshell and white Persian.

breeds, is never difficult if attended to every few days. A cat will live to maybe 20 years of age, which is more than with most dogs. Its initial cost can vary from nothing to quite a lot of money, but even a good-quality kitten with show potential will not be as expensive as its equivalent in dogs or the larger parrots.

It is because of these many virtues that cat owning has increased steadily over the last few years - more so than with most other pets. The trend is likely to continue because, apart from new owners, the facts indicate that previous first-time owners will obtain a second and even a third kitten

TFH Publications, the publisher of this book, is the largest publisher of cat books in the world. Write for a free catalogue to TFH, free catalogue, Box 427, Neptune, NJ 07753. In the United Kingdom, write to TFH, PO Box 15, Waterlooville, PO7 6BQ.

Chocolate Havana.

You can take a cat out of the wild, but you can't take the wild out of a cat.

Cats can live for up to 20 years.

## ACCOMMODATION

Kittens are social animals...three are three times as much fun as one.

within a year of having the first one. This in itself tells you that once you have a kitty, you will probably be hooked on them and want another, which is actually a very good idea.

In this small book, you will find all the basic information needed to ensure you obtain a nice kitten and are able to provide for all its needs in such a way that it will lead a healthy and contented life.

Sorrel Abyssinian female, grand champion, 11 months old.

The cat in the foreground is angry. You can tell by the arched back and bristly fur.

A black and white Persian.

## Accommodation

Kittens are really easy to cater to in respect to their housing needs. Even if you provide a specific bed, they may still choose to sleep in all sorts of places - cats are just made that way. More often than not they will choose a given chair or will sleep on your bed if you will allow this. Even so, it is always best to provide them with their own sleeping quarters so they can decide where they want to spend each night.

They will certainly be encouraged to use a basket or similar bed if this is placed above ground level. This is because they are, by nature, animals that prefer the feeling of security that comes with being off the ground. The young kitten will of course not wish to be far from the floor because it will not be able to jump well until it is about four or more months of age.

# ACCOMMODATION

**Choice of Beds**

The least expensive type of bed you can provide would simply be a cut-down stiff cardboard box lined with paper and a soft blanket material. However, a cardboard box will not remain useable for any great length of time. If you wish to obtain a really good bed, there are many manufactured just for cats.

The Cat-A-Lac from Designer Products is a sturdy, durable cat carrier. It is reuseable and easily folds for storage.

Cats like to prowl and catch small animals like rats and mice...and birds, too.

The best material is fiberglass because it is easy to clean and provides no niches for fleas, lice or other crawlies to hide in. It can be lined with a blanket or cushion, which should be washed on a regular basis. Plastic cat beds are fine, but they may get scratched. Wicker baskets are popular but will need regular attention to keep them clean. Dirt can accumulate in between the cane strands - as can fecal matter and anything regurgitated by the kitten if the entire basket is not fully covered with a suitable material. Another excellent bed would be a cat-carrying box. As with all beds, it must be large enough for the adult cat to stretch out in, as well as to stand up in, in this particular instance. The major advantage of the carry box is that it enables you to place the kitten in it whenever you wish to restrict its movements around the house - such as at night during the first few days after you have obtained it. Also, it is very useful to us when taking the kitten to the vet, or later when you go on vacation, assuming you plan to take the kitty

Cats sometimes hunt in packs...just like lions.

A black smoke Persian.

# ACCOMMODATION

Your local pet shop has dozens of different cat books published by TFH. There is a TFH cat book to suit the needs of every cat owner.

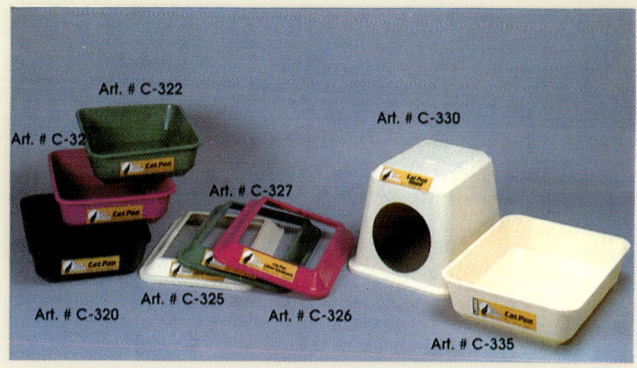

Hagen cat litter pans and houses are available from your local pet shop. The numbers indicate the catalogue numbers assigned by Hagen and are meaningful to your pet shop operator.

Nilodor® makes an odor and stain eliminator called Natural Touch, which is perfect for removing the stains and odors generated by kittens.

The ideal book for the new kitten owner. Get a copy at your local pet shop.

Most cat litter pans can be fitted with Hagen liners, which make changing the litter very easy and sanitary.

with you. All cat owners should own a carrying box, which can be purchased from your local pet store. Do be sure its dimensions are generous, as many owners buy one suited to the kitten, which they continue to squeeze the poor cat into long after it has outgrown it!

## Litter Tray

You will need a litter tray for your kitten. Cats are very clean animals and are easily trained to use their tray. Some are simple plastic trays; others have guards around them so that the kitty will not scratch the litter over the edges. Yet others are igloo types that provide a sense of security to the cat and minimize any toilet smells. Litter comes in many grades, but it is best to purchase

# ACCOMMODATION

those that neutralize odors. You will need the tray once the kitty is a few months old, and assuming you let it out daily. It will then attend to its needs in the garden and will diligently cover up any urine or feces, so it really is a very clean pet to have. Once your cat is litter trained, you can take the tray with you on vacation, and your cat will then never soil motel rooms or any other places.

## Grooming Aids

If you have a shorthaired breed, you will need only a medium-soft brush and a fine-toothed comb. If the kitten is a longhair, then purchase a double-sided comb (medium or fine/wide). Avoid cheap combs and brushes because they generate static electricity, which causes the hair to 'fly away,' meaning it stands off the lie of the coat. Groom the longhaired kitten daily so it gets used

A sepia agouti tabby Singapura.

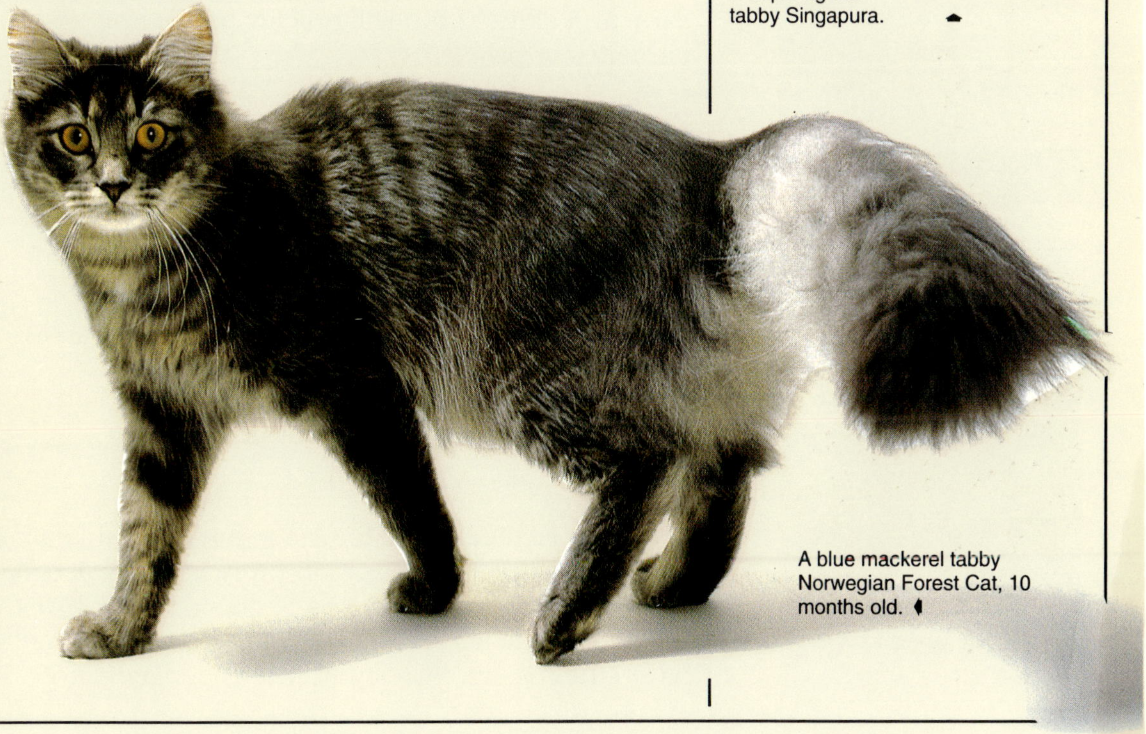

A blue mackerel tabby Norwegian Forest Cat, 10 months old.

## ACCOMMODATION

Hagen makes a complete line of Salon Soft Stroke comb and brush sets specifically manufactured for cats. These are available through your local pet shop.

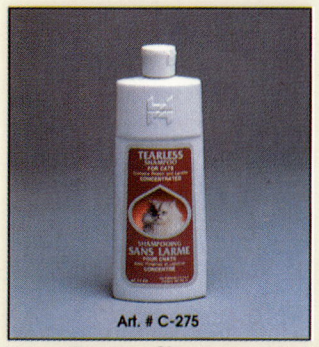

Hagen Tearless Shampoo protects your kitten's eyes from irritation during bathing.

Hagen Flea and Tick Shampoo keeps your kitten free of external parasites.

to this - but be especially gentle on its underparts and tail. Othwerwise, it will dislike being groomed. Tease out any tangles with your fingers before grooming. Whilst attending the fur, you can take the opportunity to check over the kitten's teeth, ears, and skin so you will quickly notice any parasites or problems.

### Feeding Dishes

Your pet shop will have a wide range of dishes suited to cats. Those in aluminum or crock will be more expensive than the plastic ones but will give much longer service and are easy to clean. You can purchase sophisticated types which have plastic covers which open when the cat stands on the footplate, and you can purchase double dishes. You will want one dish for water and one for food, with maybe a third for dry foods.

### Playthings

Kittens really do love to play games, and it is a vital part of their socialization process. Your pet shop will have many cat toys to choose from, but select only the better ones that are not likely to be bitten into easily. Swallowed pieces of plastic are

# ACCOMMODATION

Select only toys made especially for cats. Hagen specializes in such toys, samples of which are shown here.

potentially lethal to kittens. Many items in your home will also make ideal toys. The cardboard from used toilet rolls, old cotton reel bobbins, and ping pong balls suspended on string to a post are examples of items that your kitten will really enjoy playing with. They love to clamber in and out of cardboard boxes.

**Scratching Post**

If you do not want your kitten to get into the

There are literally hundreds of toys you can buy for your cat. Photo courtesy of Hagen.

Hagen *Sunbow Balls* are intriguing to kittens.

A tortoiseshell and white Japanese Bobtail.

habit of scratching your furniture and carpets, you should purchase a scratching post. This is simply a pillar which is clad in carpet. It can be free standing (on a heavy base so it does not topple over when used), or it can be screwed to a suitable wall. If you place the kitten against it and draw two front feet down the post, it will soon get the idea. Suspending a ball on a string from it will encourage its use and serve as a toy.

# ACCOMMODATION

The Hagen Sisal Scratcher is a rope-covered cat scratching post that saves the drapes and furniture.

## Cat Doors

If you wish your kitten to have freedom to come and go when it pleases (once it is mature), then you can fit a cat door to an outside door. There are numerous models to choose from, but the best are those which give you a range of options, and are

A blue smoke Persian.

also fitted with magnetic strips so they do not open when it is windy (thus causing drafts). You can install them so that they open outwards, inwards, or both ways. Their disadvantage if allowing kitty in at will is that he or she may return with a mouse it has caught - or toms may enter if you have an in-heat female.

A seal lynx-point American Curl.

# CHOOSING A KITTEN

## Choosing a Kitten

One of the great advantages of obtaining a kitten as compared to a puppy is that if you choose to have a mixed-breed kitty, there will be no problem in wondering just how large it will grow to become. All cats, regardless of whether they are purebred or moggies, will mature to a size that varies little. Such variation is so insignificant that you can ignore the size factor, it being a case that some will be a little larger than others. Your consideration will therefore be whether to have a purebred or not and how to tell if the kitten is healthy.

The *Hagen Self-groomer* allows the cat to massage itself and lose its loose hairs.

A red Abyssinian female grand champion.

 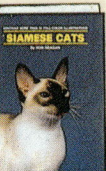

TFH publishes breed-specific books on the most popular breeds of cat. See them at your local pet shop.

## Purebred or Moggie?

If you plan to exhibit or breed cats, then you will need a purebred kitten. You may also have seen a particular breed of cat which especially appeals to you even though it is only to be a house pet. If you want just a nice kitten, then many moggies, meaning kittens of a mixed ancestry, can be very beautiful and individual in their colors and markings.

All cats are individuals in respect to their personalities, much being determined by the way they are cared for. However, certain breeds do tend to exhibit characteristics which are coupled to their breed type. These are discussed in the final chapter of this book which reviews a sampling of breeds.

A silver classic tabby American Shorthair.

9

# CHOOSING A KITTEN

Shorthaired cats require minimal grooming, even if they are allowed outdoors.

A blue and white Persian.

Cats are very observant; and if they meet someone they don't recognize, they never take their eyes away from them.

## Coat Length

An important consideration is that of coat length. If you are the sort who does not have a great deal of time to devote to grooming your pet, then choose a shorthaired kitten. Some breeds, such as the Persian, will quickly look a mess if they are not groomed daily. Their fur will collect all

A black Persian.

manner of debris, such as grasses, twigs, and burrs. When it rains, their fur will tangle as it dries and mats will form, so all in all, they are only suited to those prepared to manage their coats. Some breeds, such as the Birman, have a coat of medium length, so you will find there are many breeds from which to choose based on your particular needs. Even shorthaired breeds will need to be groomed, but the time devoted to this will be minimal; if a week or two is missed they will still retain their immaculate appearance.

## Where to Obtain Your Kitten

Pet shops stock kittens, and for many would-be cat owners, this is a good place to start. However, a pet shop cannot possibly stock every available cat breed. If your pet shop dealer does not have the particular cat breed that you want, perhaps he can refer you to another source. For example, catteries, whose business it is to breed show-quality cats, sometimes have extra cats for

# CHOOSING A KITTEN

sale. Additionally, you might check the ads in the national cat magazines as well as contacting one of the many breed clubs.

## Selecting a Healthy Kitten

Your first guide to the health of a kitten is to watch it as it plays. It should move about with no indication of having problems, such as a limp. It will appear lively and not show disinterest in what is going on around it. A kitten that comes to you boldly is always a good sign. Once satisfied that it appears healthy at a distance, you can then pick it up and inspect it more carefully. 1. The eyes should be round, clear and exhibit no signs of weeping or staining of the fur around the eye. 2. The nose should be damp and not wet or exhibiting any swellings. 3. The ears should smell sweet and be clean inside. 4. The teeth should be white and neatly aligned. They will, of course, be very small. 5. The body should be plump without being pot-bellied, which would suggest worms or some other intestinal problem. There should be no swellings or abrasions on the skin. 6. The fur will not have the high-gloss sheen of the adult cat, but it should still look healthy. There should be no bald patches anywhere. Use your hand to brush the fur against its lie. This will allow you to see the skin. If parasites are present, such as fleas, they will scurry away as you brush the fur. Slow-moving dark-gray insects are lice. Neither parasite is a sign of good management. 7. The anal region should be clean with no indication of stains or congealed fecal matter. 8. There should be no kinks in the tail.

A champion male Sphynx.

A champion male fawn Somali.

## CHOOSING A KITTEN

If you are purchasing an expensive purebred kitten, you would be wise to request it comes with a written veterinary certificate of health. It should also have been vaccinated against the major feline diseases at least 7 days before you collect it.

A tortoiseshell and white Japanese Bobtail.

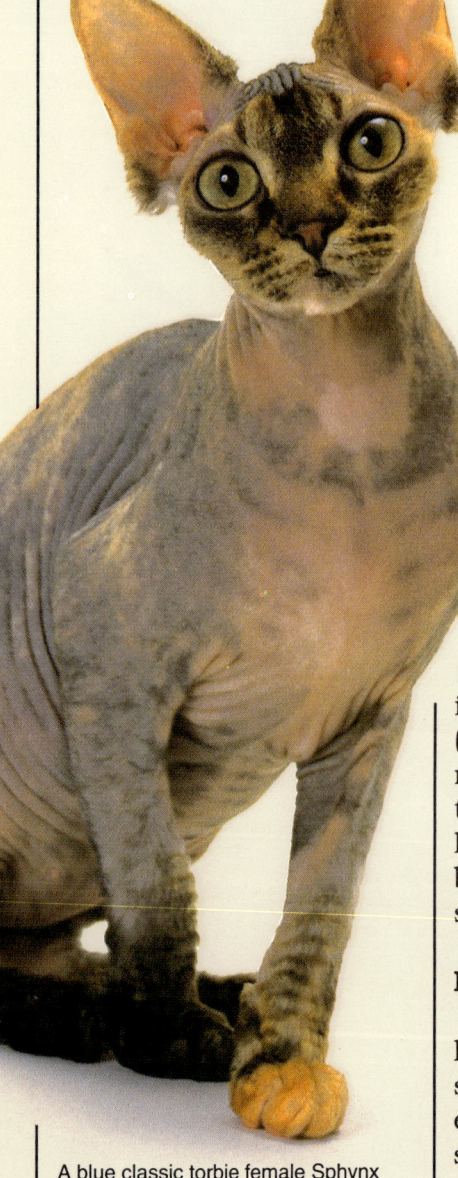

A blue classic torbie female Sphynx kitten.

### Which sex?

If the kitten is to be purely a pet, then it really makes no difference which sex you have. Both will make affectionate companions and both will need surgical attention in the form of neutering so they are unable to breed. This is very important with pet kittens. An unneutered male (tom) will spray around the home and will also be more likely to go off fighting all the other males in the area. The unneutered female (queen) will be in heat constantly, thus producing more unwanted babies to add to the already excessive numbers of such kittens.

### Registration

If it is your desire to exhibit your purebred kitten when it is old enough, then you must be sure it is bred from registered parents and is thus eligible itself to be registered. The breeder should supply evidence of this and, of course, all of the necessary paperwork, such as transfer forms and pedigree. You can, however, exhibit non-purebred

# FEEDING KITTY

kittens in classes specifically for pet cats. Such classes also cater to purebreds which are not eligible for registration. Some breeds are not able to compete in championship classes because they have only provisional acceptance of breeds. Those interested in exhibition are advised to obtain a copy of *The Atlas of Cats of the World* by Dennis Kelsey-Wood (TFH Publications). This work covers all aspects of showing, both in Britain and in the USA, as well as giving excellent detail on every breed of cat.

A white Devon Rex.

Dennis Kelsey-Wood's classic best-seller is available through every pet shop.

## Feeding Kitty

Cats are prime carnivores, meaning they are flesh-eaters that are natural predators in the wild state. Their diet must reflect this fact, even more so than with dogs. With a predatory animal, you must appreciate that its whole digestive system has evolved to cope with a given form of nutrition. If this is not supplied, then the kitten will not grow as healthy, or as well, as it should. A carnivore cannot digest vegetable matter very well because its gut does not contain the kind of microbacteria needed to break down the tough cellulose walls of such food as do cows, sheep and animals evolved to live on vegetation.

The wild cat obtains its vegetable matter via the stomach contents of its prey. So, it does need plant matter—but only if this is partly digested or lightly cooked so it can be absorbed ito the cat's system. The various microbacteria found in the gut of meat eaters are specific to these animals. A byproduct of their metabolism are certain vitamins which are essential to the health of your kitten. Correct feeding is thus a very complex matter. However, as long as you understand the very basics of feline

A chocolate point Siamese.

13

## FEEDING KITTY

A red classic tabby American Shorthair.

A chocolate Burmese.

nutrition, you will be able to ensure your kitten has all of the needed foods to create a balanced diet. Fortunately, most cat owners today feed their pets on canned foods that have been commercially prepared to extremely high standards of content. They are complete - all you need to be sure of is that you have a can opener!

### The Composition of Food

Food is comprised of chemical compounds held together in very definite configurations. These form the basic categories of food which you will probably know something about.

*Proteins.* These are the building blocks of the body. Kittens need plenty of proteins so they can develop sound muscles and internal organs. Tissue is constantly being worn out by the kitten's activities so protein is needed so new tissue can replace this. A kitten of 6-9 months of age will be consuming more protein than a fully mature cat.

*Water.* All foods contain some water, and it is also a byproduct of cell metabolism. Cats are able to survive on minimal water intake better than dogs because they can adjust the water loss of

A seal point Ragdoll, male, grand champion.

# FEEDING KITTY

their bodies and urine. However, it should always be available to them - and it should be fresh each day. This is especially true if they are fed dry complete foods, as the water content in these is extremely low.

## How Much to Feed

The daily quantity of food required by your kitten will be dependent on a number of factors: the temperature, the size of the kitten, its activity level and the quality of the food given. In cold climates, the kitten will need more than in places that are warm. This is because so much of the food is needed to provide insulation against the cold, which obviously is not as applicable in warm climates. A large breed, such as the Maine Coon, will clearly eat more than a small Siamese or its like. An active kitten will burn up a lot of energy if it has access to an interesting garden - as compared with an apartment kitten that spends most of its time sleeping and doing very little that is strenuous (such as climbing trees). Finally, the better the quality of the food the less of it will be needed to meet your kitten's full nutritional needs.

Given these interacting considerations and the fact that each kitten's appetite, even for the same-sized cat, can vary considerably, it is best not to feed specific weights of food. Use a common-sense approach. Feed the kitten only what it will consume at a single sitting. Any that is left can be placed in the refrigerator for the next meal, or discarded—depending on how much is left. You will quickly come to know how much to feed. If the kitty eats all you give it and is looking for more, then give a little more until it is satiated. Most animals, including most cats, rarely eat more than they need.

## How Often to Feed

The following is a guideline to the needs of the

CAT LOVE by Hagen is a suitable treat for cats.

Your cat should have its own dish. The dish must be cleaned after each meal. This style of dish is very good because it can't be tipped over.

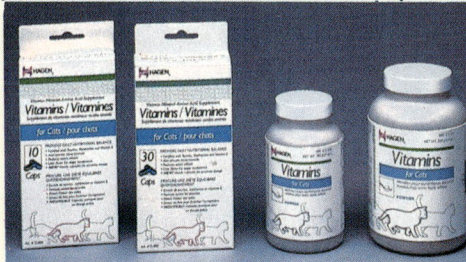

Hagen makes special vitamins for cats.

Hagen Dried Fish is a real treat for cats.

15

## FEEDING KITTY

This Singapura is overfed, overweight and under-exercised.

A brown classic tabby Maine Coon kitten.

average kitten. Whenever possible feed on the basis of a little but often - this is how small cats eat in the wild.

Age/Meals per Day: Up to 12 weeks, 5-6. Three can be meat meals and the rest milk and cereal; 12-16 weeks, 4-5. Three meat and 1-2 milk and cereal; 16-26 weeks, 4, 2-3 meat and 1-2 milk and cereal. 26-52 weeks, 3-4, 2 meat and 1-2 milk and cereal. Over 52 weeks, 2-3, meat.

As you reduce the number of meat meals, you must increase the quantity given at the remaining meals so that the cat grows well and with good muscle. The milk/cereal meals are not that important as the kitten grows because in the wild it would receive milk only during its early life. As the kitten grows, be sure the milk is diluted because it can have too much of this and the result will be an upset stomach.

**The Balanced Diet**

For a well-rounded diet, never feed the same foods day after day. The greater the variety your kitten receives the less chance there will be of any important ingredient being missing. There will also be less chance of the kitten becoming a faddy eater, though it will clearly have given preferences and dislikes. At all times the general health and condition of its coat are your best guide to how well it is being fed. If you have any doubts on this matter you should consult your veterinarian, or, of course, an experienced cat owner if there is one near you, which there usually is.

# A Kitten in the Home

If you have followed the advice in this book, then you will have already obtained all the needed items for the kitten and will have selected a nice healthy one. Collect it as early in the day as possible so it has plenty of time to explore its new home before you retire for the night. Be sure to obtain a copy of its feeding regimen from the seller. It is best to transport the kitten in a proper carrying box, but if someone is to hold it on their lap in your car, then they should place a towel on this in case the kitten is sick. On a long journey be sure you have some water to give to it, and maybe some dry cat food. It will also need its litter tray to go to the toilet.

Once home, you should let it explore those rooms it will be allowed into - ours have full freedom of the house. It will soon be wanting a nap so place it in its basket or its lined carry box. Do not let children pester it or play for too long with it. Kittens quickly tire. It will no doubt appreciate a light meal and a drink. When you go to bed, place the kitty in its basket and include a cuddly toy if you only have the one kitten. It will miss its littermates for the first night or two, and a toy will give it something to cuddle up to. You may of course let it sleep on your bed, which will please it greatly - but only do this if you intend to continue doing so as it grows.

### Dangers in the Home

Kittens are very inquisitive so you must be sure that potential dangers are guarded against. The more common of these are **1**. Any wires trailing from tables that the kitten might attempt to climb up - pulling lamps or electric items on to them. **2**. The wire from an iron in use - if this hit the kitty it would probably kill it. **3**. Open washing machines or dryer doors. Kittens love to snuggle up in clothes and this could end in disaster if you do not

A Russian blue female.

TFH has books on specific groups of cats...like *Long-haired Cats*. This and other TFH books are available from your local pet supplier.

## A KITTEN IN THE HOME

notice the kitty asleep. **4.** Open fires. Kittens are aware that fires are dangerous, but even so they could be burned by a hot piece of wood or coal that sparked out of the fire. Always fit a fire guard. **5.** Hot gas rings or hobs. The kitchen is potentially very dangerous to a kitten, yet it is a room they will no doubt spend much time in. As they grow, do not let them jump on work surfaces as they might get badly burned - or cause you to be. When very little they can easily get under your feet and you just might be carrying a pan of boiling water or a hot frying pan. **6.** Be sure any fish tanks have a canopy or hood fitted to them as more than one kitten has drowned due to its curious nature. **7.** Be sure all balconies are protected with mesh - at least until the kitten has matured and is more aware of dangers. **8.** Be watchful of through drafts created by open doors and windows as these could cause a door to slam on the kitten.

**9.** Do not leave any toxic substances where a kitten might chew or lick on them. It is also wise to remove any valuable and fragile collectibles from any shelves which the kitten just might be able to jump onto!

**Litter Training**

Kittens are extremely clean creatures in their personal habits, so litter training is easy if a few basic rules are observed. Your kitten will want to attend its toilet needs many times a day. As it grows, it will be more able to control its bowel movements and will use its toilet less. After a meal, after it wakes up, and after play periods are the prime times it will want to relieve itself. A kitten will cry and start looking around for a suitable place to attend to its needs and you must watch for these signs. Lift the kitten up and place it into the litter

A seal point Himalayan.

A brown classic tabby Maine Coon kitten.

# A KITTEN IN THE HOME

tray and hold it there for a few moments. It will paw at the litter and attend its needs. If it does nothing and jumps out of the tray, simply place it back and repeat.

After just one or two such sessions it will automatically use its tray - though still being a baby there may be the odd accident when it does not use the tray. This may be because the tray was not easily accessible or was too dirty. Cats do not like using previously fouled trays, so clean these after each use. As it gets older it will attend its needs in the garden, and the tray can be stored, to be used on vacations or if the cat has to be kept in the home for any reason.

## General Training

Your kitten should understand its name, so use this frequently. It will then come on hearing it (usually!), especially at meal times. You cannot teach a cat like you can a dog, but fortunately they do not create the same problems. If they are doing something they shouldn't, just say 'no' in a firm voice and they will invariably respond. If they do not then clap your hands and this will do the trick. If they are walking on shelves where they might damage something, do not startle them into flight. Walk calmly up to them and lift them off. There are rarely occasions when they will actually need a slap and this should never be more than a light smack on their rump. This is sufficient to get the message across - but it must be done at the moment of the misdemeanor and never after a lapse of even a few moments. Otherwise, they will not relate it to the incident.

## Grooming

Your kitten should be groomed daily from the time you obtain it. By attending this need the kitten will never become difficult to handle - an important point later in life when visiting the vet

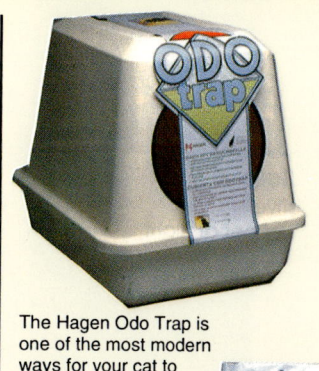

The Hagen Odo Trap is one of the most modern ways for your cat to relieve itself and for you to control odors.

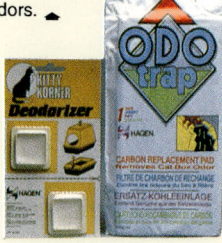

The secret of the Odo Trap is a carbon filter that absorbs odor.

An alternative to the Odo Trap is the open-top litter tray.

You can remove dried feces from the litter with special spoons.

19

# A KITTEN IN THE HOME

Your local pet shop has Hagen's LE SALON, from which you can select your own grooming tools.

Hagen Nylon Cat Collars are available in a number of stylish designs.

for example. Be gentle when brushing or combing the underbelly and the tail, as these are very sensitive areas. Even shorthaired breeds are better for being groomed daily, and such cats will not take long to do. Inspect the kitten's fur, teeth and ears as you attend the grooming.

## Lead Training

Cats do not take kindly to lead training, though some breeds such as Foreigns and Siamese seem more willing to walk on a lead than others. Actually a cat harness is a better proposition than a collar if the cat is taken out of its own home area (which is your garden). Place the harness on the kitten for short periods each day so it becomes familiar with its feel. When this causes it no concern, you can then attach a light lead and walk the kitten in your garden so it gets used to the restriction. It is a much slower process than with dogs, and I stress that the average cat will never feel happy on a lead unless it is taken out very regularly - even then it will be uneasy in unknown territory. Be sure the area is quiet and free from roaming dogs, which would quickly panic the cat.

## Handling

Handle your kitten often and gently. Never pick it up by the scruff of its neck, as you may see some people do - this is quite wrong. Support its chest and stomach on your arm and against your chest, leaving your other hand free to secure it or stroke it. Some kittens will grow up to dislike being lifted up, even if they were handled gently as kittens; others will love it, and yet others will be happy to be lifted and fussed over only when they (not you) are in the mood for such. This is just the nature of cats and why they have the reputation for being very aloof, even unsocial at times. It is this

## A KITTEN IN THE HOME

independent aspect of their personalities that gives them so much appeal to all genuine cat lovers. If you cannot accept this aspect of the adult cat, you should choose a puppy for a pet and not a kitten.

Some kittens like dogs better than people. Dogs are much friendlier pets than cats...but they are also more dependent upon their owners for care.

This is a brown classic tabby and white male Maine Coon double grand champion.

## KEEPING KITTENS HEALTHY

# Keeping Kittens Healthy

Given care to its day-to-day needs, your kitten should experience few illnesses, these normally being restricted to off days, minor colds, stomach upsets and the sort of little ailments that befall us all. If you ignore the signs of illness, these could develop into serious, maybe fatal, diseases.

**Vaccinations**

Your first line of defense against the major feline-killer diseases is in ensuring your kitten is protected by vaccinations. These are normally given when the kitten is about 9 weeks of age. A booster is then given about 3-4 weeks later. Prior to being vaccinated, and for a week after the booster, the kitten should be kept in the home so the risk of it contracting disease via airborne germs or by direct contact with other cats is minimal. Contact your vet as soon as you get the

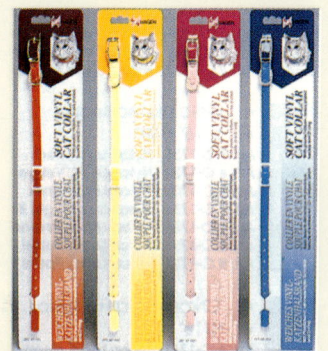

Hagen Nylon Stretch Collars are practical for cats allowed outdoors. The collar can't choke the cat if it gets hooked on a branch or some such object.

For long-haired breeds, the Hagen Soft Vinyl Cat Collar is must.

Special Hagen Break-away Cat Collars are available through your local pet shop.

A blue tortoiseshell smoke Persian female.

# KEEPING KITTENS HEALTHY

kitten so an appointment can be made to have the vaccinations attended to. Your vet will detail those which he or she advises you to have done. These will usually be for protection against cat flu (feline influenza), feline infectious enteritis and rabies (depending on the country you live in). Feline leukemia virus is another disease that can now be treated by vaccine.

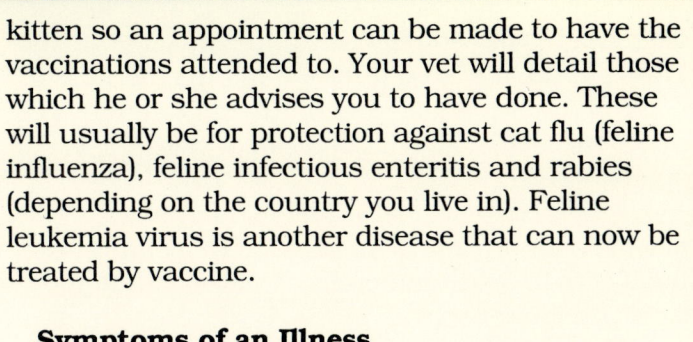

These and many other cat books by TFH are available at your local pet shop.

### Symptoms of an Illness

Most illnesses and diseases invariably exhibit some physical signs that should alert you to a problem. If these do not clear up within 36 hours, you should contact your veterinarian so that no time is lost that will allow the problem to increase its progress. Unfortunately, there are no differences in the early symptoms of a major disease than of a minor upset, which is why a delay in responding to symptoms can be a

A red classic tabby Persian female.

# KEEPING KITTENS HEALTHY

A Russian Blue.

A shaded golden Persian.

A particolor point Cornish Rex.

dilemma to you, so play safe and contact your vet. This is especially true if the symptoms increase in severity and progress from one symptom to two or more. All of the following indicate something is amiss.

*1. Diarrhea* - especially if it is streaked with blood. A minor tummy upset (due to a change in the diet) will result in soft fecal matter but liquid feces are more serious.

*2. Weeping eyes and a runny nose.* These could indicate a minor chill, in which case they will clear up rapidly if the kitten is kept in a warm room. If the condition persists and gets worse, then it is more than a chill.

*3. Vomiting.* It is normal for cats to vomit periodically, especially after they have chewed on grass. However, persistent vomiting is not normal. There may be a blockage in the intestinal tract, due to hairballs in longhaired breeds, or it may be for many other reasons.

*4. Loss of appetite.* All cats have their off days; but if the kitten has shown no interest in its food over a 12-hour period, something may be wrong. If it is drinking abnormal amounts of water, something is very wrong.

*5. Abnormal breathing.* You will not be able to hear your cat breathing if it is healthy. If you hear a wheezing sound, this indicates a respiratory problem. In hot weather, or after much exertion, your kitten may pant. In this case place it in a cool and quiet spot so it can quickly recover.

*6. Scratching.* All cats enjoy a good scratch, but this should not be excessive, or such that it results in abrasions. This would indicate a parasitic attack, not in itself a major problem, but which could result in secondary infection. Groom the kitten and treat for the causal parasite - do not forget to treat or destroy the kitten's bedding (blanket, toweling or such).

# KEEPING KITTENS HEALTHY

A blue mackerel tabby Norwegian Forest Cat female.

## Treating Illness

Before an illness can be treated it must first be accurately diagnosed. If it is not, then time is wasted in treating for the wrong problem, which will actually make matters worse. This so, do not attempt home remedies. Let your vet deal with the problem. Your role is to ensure that the vet's instructions are followed to the letter. Do not discontinue a treatment because the kitten seems to have improved. This could result in a relapse. Always remember that warmth and quiet are two of nature's finest cures for minor conditions and will often prevent such a condition developing into a major one.

## Minor Cuts and Abrasions

Although kittens and cats are inquisitive and explore in some potentially dangerous places, they seem remarkably adept at avoiding being cut. However, should your kitten receive a minor cut, then all that is usually necessary is to bath the wound and then apply an antiseptic ointment. In the event of a bad wound, then wrap the kitten carefully in a towel, both to keep it warm and to stem the flow of blood. Transport it quickly to the vet for treatment. In all instances of accidents, you should remain calm and try to make the patient comfortable without risking too much movement to its limbs or head.

A black Oriental Shorthair.

A ruddy Abyssinian.

25

# WHICH BREED?

A classic tabby Manx.

A black and white Manx.

A red classic tabby and white Maine Coon.

## Which Breed?

Cats are relatively uniform in their conformation when compared to dogs, horses, rabbits and other popular domesticated pets. As a result, the distinction between the breeds is more subtle. For example, color or coat length is sufficient to raise a cat to breed status, whereas in dogs these would merely be variations within a breed. However, in broad terms, cats can be divided into two basic categories. 1. Longhairs. These vary from the profusely coated Persian (called simply Longhaired in the UK) to the silky and less dense coat of breeds such as the Balinese. None can be described as natural breeds because there are no naturally longcoated wild cats. They are therefore all the result of the long coat mutation being transferred to shorhaired breeds. 2. Shorthairs. These represent about two-thirds of all cat breeds. Some may be regarded as natural breeds in that they have been recognized for very many years; others are the result of hybridization and mutations that have appeared in breeds and been retained and improved by selective breeding. The shorthairs can be divided into two basic body forms. a) The cobby type of breed with good muscle and a good-sized round head. b) The foreign type which has a lithe body and a wedge shaped head - the Siamese type if you like.

### Some Longhaired Breeds

The most popular longhaired cat is the Persian. Its fur is profuse and its face just slightly dished. It is a quiet breed seen in either a single color, such as white, black, blue, and red, or it may be bicolored, pointed (dark extremities) or of varying shades of the same color as seen in smokes and cameos. Its coat will need very regular grooming. In some USA registries, the Himalayan (a colorpointed cat) is given breed status, but in most

# WHICH BREED?

other societies it is regarded as a color pointed Persian (Colourpoint Longhair in the UK).

The Balinese will appeal to those who like the Siamese but prefer a longhaired cat - this breed is a longhaired Siamese. If the colors are not as for the Siamese, then it is another breed - the Javanese (but in the UK all colors are still regarded as Balinese). With less fur and a more normal nose shape than the Persian is the Birman. This gorgeous breed sports white gauntlets (rear) and gloves or mittens (front) on its feet. It may be blue, seal, chocolate or lilac in color - this contrasting on the body with darker extremities (mask, ears, tail and lower legs).

If you like a big longhaired cat, then the Maine Coon should suit you. This old American breed is regaining its former popularity and deservedly so. In tabby pattern or black, it is a very striking cat that has retained the ruggedness of a breed that had to survive in the cold climates of Maine. Other colors are also available. Very similar is the Norwegian Forest and the even larger Siberian, the latter a new breed in the USA that is sure to appeal to 'big' cat lovers.

A longhaired breed which has easily managed fur is the Somali. This is a beautiful breed and is the longhaired version of the famous Abyssinian. The coat is a reddish color with black ticking, and the breed is extremely intelligent. It does enjoy outdoor exercise so is best suited to those with gardens. Two closely related longhaired breeds are the Angora and the Turkish Van. The first named was originally all white, whilst the Van was white with auburn markings. It is from Turkish cats like these that the Persian was developed. Today, the Angora and the Van are seen in numerous colors. The coat is silky and, not having the profuse undercoat of the Persian, is much easier to keep tidy.

A seal point Himalayan.

A brown mackerel tabby Maine Coon.

A seal point Siamese.

27

# WHICH BREED?

A brown classic tabby Manx.

## Some Shorthaired Breeds

Two of the most popular shorthaired breeds are the British and American Shorthairs, the latter having been developed from the cats brought to America by the early settlers. Both are natural breeds - your original street cats that were tough and unaltered by fashion. However, they have been selectively bred for many years, and quality examples are far removed from your average alley cat in terms of their pureness of colors and markings. Tabby markings in these breeds are seen at their very best and may be

A tortoiseshell Oriental Shorthair.

either classic or mackerel. Some American shorthairs have a look of Persian in their faces, and this is because the latter breed was crossed with them for a while, but most has now been bred out. However, from these

A red mackerel tabby Cornish Rex.

28

## WHICH BREED?

crosses arose the Exotic Shorthair, which is now a breed in itself. It is judged to the Persian standard but has a short dense coat. Both the British and American shorthairs have been used in the creation of other breeds.

A very distinct breed is the Manx, or tailless, cat. Actually, a number do have tails, albeit much reduced in size. The breed is associated with certain anatomical problems, as the tailless mutation is variably lethal. This so, prospective owners should be aware of potential conditions that might be encountered. A longhaired variety of the breed is called the Cymric. If you like short tailed cats, but which have no associated problems, the Japanese Bobtail is possibly the breed for you. It is lively, intelligent and slim, without being skinny.

If you like an all-blue cat, then look over the Russian Blue or the Korat. Both are impressive. The Chartreux of France, and, of course, the famous British Blue, complete a quartet of cats with truly beautiful blue coats with a tinge of silver to them. A very old established breed is the Abyssinian. The original color of this breed was a red agouti: red ticked with black and yellow -

A fawn Somali.

A tortoiseshell Persian.

A calico Persian female kitten.

29

## WHICH BREED?

white. Nowadays you can also have a blue agouti, and in the UK chocolate, silver, lilac and others. It is a lithe and athletic breed that will appeal to the discerning cat lover. Somewhat similar, but a very recent arrival on the cat scene, is the Singapura.

Everyone will know of the Siamese. This slim, wedge-faced breed is both intelligent and vocal. It is almost doglike in

A seal point Siamese female.

A lilac point Siamese male grand champion.

# WHICH BREED?

many of its characteristics, so is well suited to those who want a cat that will be very involved in the family. Less popular, but with similar characteristics, is the Burmese. It has a little more muscle on it than the Siamese but is still a slim cat. Its colors are sable brown, champagne (chocolate), platinum (lilac) and blue. The UK accepts other colors, but these are not recognized in the USA. You may hear of Colorpoint Shorthairs and Oriental Shorthairs. These are Siamese in either pointed colors not accepted as Siamese, or they are self-colored Siamese. In the UK, the self-colored Siamese are referred to as Foreign: black, white or whatever color they happen to be. The Havana brown breed is lovely deep brown and is Siamese in its type.

A natural mink Tonkinese.

Two breeds with very attractive spotted coats are the Egyptian Mau and the Ocicat - both are gaining new followers every year and are indeed most attractive. Another handsome breed is the Snowshoe. This is a hybrid resulting from crossing Siamese with bicolored American Shorthairs. Its color is similar to the Birman but with short hair. It is also rather variable in its type, as it is one of numerous new breeds still being developed.

A fawn spotted tabby Oriental Shorthair.

There are many other breeds from which you can choose, but exercise caution with those associated with genetic problems of the coat (such as the almost-hairless Sphynx) or of the ears (the Scottish Fold), as these could present you with problems. On the other hand, coats such as seen in the Rex breeds (Cornish or Devon) are unusual yet not linked to abnormal

A blue and white bicolor male Persian.

31

## WHICH BREED?

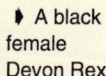

▶ A black female Devon Rex.

◆ *THE ALLURE OF THE CAT* is probably the most beautiful cat book ever published. In a competition with over 100,000 books conducted by *GOOD HOUSEKEEPING MAGAZINE*, this book was selected as the number one best Christmas gift book for 1993.

Your local pet shop has all of the books shown on this page and dozens of other TFH cat books from which you can gather dependable information. ◆◆

problems. If you really want to see a full range of breeds from which to choose, I would certainly recommend you take the time to visit a major cat show. You will be amazed just how many breeds there are which will really appeal to you, many of which you will never have seen or heard of before.